TO:_____

FROM_____

I love you because you are

The very best thing about you is

I adore the feel of your

You look fantastic when you wear

The expression on your
face was delightful when

You make me strive to be a better

I'm kind of obsessed
with your

If you were an
animal you'd be a

You deserve to

If you wanted to, you could easily

I'll always

remember when you

I have unforgettable
memories of the time we

It's very funny
when you

I'd like to take you to

I really enjoy hearing
your stories about

Together, we could be
the very best

I wish we had known
each other when

You make the absolute best

I love watching you

I admired your brilliant idea when

You really inspire
me when

Thank you
for teaching
me how to

You looked stunning when

I was very proud
of you when

I think you are
amazing because

25911565R00015

Made in the USA
Middletown, DE
17 December 2018